RAINBOW VISION
JOURNAL

YELLOW

How to take control
of your personal
well-being and happiness

SHARON DAWN

Published by: Rainbow Vision Journal
                PO Box 1062, Airlie Beach, Qld, Australia 4802
                www.rainbowvisionjournal.com
                Email: smile@rainbowvisionjournal.com

Cover Design by: Sharon Dawn
Illustrations by: Sharon Dawn
Typeset by: Adam Press

ISBN Hardcover: 978-0-648-7662-7-8
ISBN Paperback: 978-0-648-7662-8-5
ISBN eBook: 978-0-6487662-9-2

 A catalogue record for this work is available from the National Library of Australia

Copyright © 2021. All rights reserved. No part of this publication may be reproduced in any manner without prior written permission from the publisher.

The information given in this journal should not be used as a substitute for professional medical advice. Any use of the information in this journal is at the reader's discretion and risk. Readers who are experiencing adverse effects from any situation arising from using this journal should seek professional counselling. Neither the author nor the publisher can be held responsible for any loss, claim or damage arising from use, or misuse, of the suggestions made in this journal.

DEDICATION

This journal is for everyone who wants to feel good about themselves as they learn to love and listen to their body.

CONTENTS

WHAT IS THE RAINBOW VISION JOURNAL?	vii
FREE GIFTS	ix
HOW TO USE THIS JOURNAL	1
I am Silent and Listen	7
Catching My Chaser Thoughts	9
Finding My Gold Nuggets	11
I am so Grateful for	13
WHERE I AM RIGHT NOW	15
Well-being and Daily Observations	17
A Look at My Week	33
How I Felt	35
How I want to Feel	37
Where do I Struggle?	39
What is My Indulgence?	41
Choosing what I Like	43
How is My Posture?	45
Creating New Habits	47
An Honest Look	49
Journal Time	50
CREATING MY PLAN	55
Visualisation Exercise	58
My Vision for Me	59
My Eating Plan	60
My Movement Plan	63
My Self-Talk	65
My Feel-Good Plan	67
My Accountability Plan	68
Journal Time	76

LET'S GET CREATIVE — 81

- Yellow Words — 82
- Yellow Thoughts — 83
- My Empowering Affirmation — 85
- Creating Space for ME Mind Map — 86
- Create a Calendar — 89
- Feel Good Technique — 90
- Creating My Mood Vision Board — 91
- Creating the New ME Vision Board — 95
- Relaxation Technique — 99
- Create a Mandala — 101
- Journal Time — 102

BRING IT ALL TOGETHER — 105

- It's Magic — 107
- Revising My Chaser Thoughts — 111
- The Magic Rewritten — 115
- 3 Action Steps — 121
- My Reward — 123
- Check In — 125
- Journal Time – Keep up the Magic — 126
- What's Next? — 131
- Draw like a Child — 132
- Write from Within — 133
- Congratulations — 181

RED — My Heart

How to follow your heart and find your bliss.

ORANGE — My Experiences

How to have awesome experiences without worrying about time or money.

YELLOW — My Well-being

How to take control of your personal well-being and happiness.

GREEN — My Abundance

How to attract money and abundance into your life.

BLUE — My Purpose

How to discover and live your true-life purpose.

INDIGO — My Awareness

How to stay in control of your thoughts and use them to empower.

VIOLET — My Connection

How to feel connected and tuned into your heart's desires.

GOLD — My Uniqueness

How to bring your life into alignment using your Rainbow Vision Steps.

What is the RAINBOW VISION JOURNAL?

The Rainbow Vision Journal is a series of eight guided workbooks that take you on a journey to discover your true self and your inner purpose.

Rainbow

Signifies new beginnings as you break through your current path, just as the sun breaks through the clouds after rain. The bridge symbolises your journey, leading you to your pot of gold.

> *Rainbows are a magical light that make us feel peaceful. They raise our energy vibration while reminding us that life is not always as we see it.*

Vision

You have the ability to imagine, to create images and to plan your future. With vision you can look within, to see your true wisdom.

Journal

A safe place where you can capture your thoughts and ideas, plan your future, and release your past. A place where you can be honest with yourself. A place where you can be creative and be your true self.

ACKNOWLEDGEMENTS

I would like to thank the people who have taught me so much. The New Thought and personal growth teachers that share their wisdom on how our thoughts create our reality and how we have the power to choose our thoughts and therefore our reality. These teachings have changed my life and it is my sincere hope that they will change your life as you work through this journal. We all have the power to choose a better life for ourselves no matter our circumstances.

FREE GIFTS

As a thank you for purchasing this journal please accept the following gifts. They are to assist and inspire you on your journey.

- Download a guided meditation to do prior to journaling. This is a quick meditation that takes you into your heart.

- Download a guided visualization to clarify your well-being
  http://www.rainbowvisionjournal.com/downloads

- Receive regular Rainbow Vision Journal emails for support and clarity on the topics discussed in this journal. All promotions and specials will be released via the email prior to release on the website and social media. To register, go to *www.rainbowvisionjournal.com* and click on the 'Subscribe' button.

- Download the Rainbow Vision Journal FREE eBook. This eBook explains the concepts behind the Rainbow Vision Journal including your inner child, energy vibration and the law of attraction. It discusses how the key to a great life is to be aware of our thoughts and feelings so we can align them to our heart's desire. *https://www.rainbowvisionjournal.com/free-ebook/*

- Join us on Facebook and Instagram and become a member of the private Facebook group. Enjoy daily journal prompts and other interesting ideas as part of your ongoing journey into self-awareness and inner connection.

   Creating Vision Journals Together and Rainbow Vision Journal

   @rainbow_vision_journal

*The simple act of smiling benefits my whole body.
It connects me to the unconditional love in my heart.*

HOW TO USE THIS JOURNAL

Life is all about choices and how we choose to look after ourselves determines the quality of our life. We may have things that challenge us, yet our quality of life actually comes from how we choose to react to those challenges each day.

YELLOW is about being aware of where you are, in this moment and accepting the choices you have made up till now, then letting go of any self-criticism and resistance as you decide to make new choices that support you better from now on.

You are going to look at how you can improve the quality of your life by finding what works best for you. We are all different and what works for one person does not always work for someone else. The trick is to find what works best for you. What makes you feel good. What makes you feel strong and what brings you down. What empowers and energizes you, regardless of your challenges.

We have the power to choose.

Have you ever really thought about the choices you are making each day, or do you run on autopilot? Maybe you eat on the run or binge eat. Maybe you sit at a desk all day and feel stiff and sore at night or lack energy. Maybe you dislike certain things about yourself and that plays regularly on your mind.

When you think of well-being you may be thinking of diets and exercise and yes these can play a big part in it, but what about how you think about yourself? This can be just as empowering or disempowering as what you eat or do.

When you eat with guilt, or to hide certain emotions, or your self-talk is negative or criticising, that is the energy you are feeding yourself. Talking to yourself in a bad way is just as harmful as eating bad food. Talking to yourself in a good way is loving yourself and as you learn to love yourself, everything changes for the better.

How do you nurture your body?

Yellow is about feeling as good as you can. Your body is your temple, it is the vessel that takes you wherever you want to go. Without it, your life is over so the better you can feel today, the better your quality of life is tomorrow. Start taking notice of what your body and your thoughts are telling you.

It really is all about choices, your choices. You get to choose how you want your life to be, and then you start making changes to reflect that. You may decide you are perfectly healthy and that is great, or you may decide that there are too many things to work on. If that is the case, then start with one thing and decide what you are prepared to do to make your life better in that one area. Make a commitment to yourself. Only you can change you.

What energy are you putting into your body each day?

Journaling connects us to our inner self. It helps us find clarity in what is really happening to us and it allows us to explore our options. In this journal, you are going to look at your current habits and see what is working for you and what is not, and then create a plan to feel better, a plan that is specifically suited to you.

Before you start your well-being journey, look through your journal to familiarise yourself with how it works. Many of the left-hand pages are there to help capture any ideas that help you clarify your thoughts. Write, scribble, draw or paste pictures. Do anything that inspires you. Anything that makes you smile or lets you play, because when you smile and when you play, your body feels good and that is the goal we are after.

The next few pages in this first section are designed for you to use regularly as you work your way through the journal. These are your support pages. I encourage you to go back to them each time you use your journal as they are immensely powerful in helping you create a richer life for yourself.

It's time to put me first.

The first page is 'I am Silent and Listen' and this is where you can make space to hear your inner guidance. When you make a commitment to start listening from within, all sorts of opportunities open to you. This is where your true happiness is, with regular practice it becomes easier for you to hear and trust in your inner guidance.

Next is a page called 'Catching My Chaser Thoughts.' This is where you write any thoughts that are disempowering to you. Sometimes when we try to form new habits we immediately have resistance with chaser thoughts like 'I can't do this', 'I don't have time to look after myself' or worse 'I am too old, too fat, too ugly, too...' As you start creating your new lifestyle plan, capture any resistance on this page. Write exactly what pops into your head, without analyzing it and near the end of the journal you will have the opportunity to revise these.

Commit to the vision of how you want to feel.

'Finding My Gold Nuggets' is where you capture any 'aha' moments. Anything that seems perfect to you that you do not want to forget. These help you to write your magic at the end of this journal and these become part of your pot of gold at the end of the rainbow.

The last page in this section is 'I am so Grateful for', where you remind yourself and give thanks for all the wonderful things in your life. Making it a daily practice to be thankful elevates your energy vibration and is a great way to start your journal practice each day. Be thankful for every day that you achieve something towards your goal. We are often quick to berate ourselves when we fail, instead, turn it around and praise yourself and be thankful for every little win you achieve each day.

The second section in this journal is called 'Where am I Now?' In this section you will take an honest snapshot of what you are doing each day as you document a normal week in your life. What you eat and drink, what exercise or movement you do, how you feel, your moods, your level of happiness, your energy levels, and your sleep patterns. You will also become aware of any thoughts that make you feel good or make you feel bad. It is especially important to capture these thoughts as they can show how you may be sabotaging your own well-being.

I take responsibility for my body.

Remember this is just for your eyes so be as honest and in-depth as you can and write as much detail as possible. There is a wealth of information for you to gain in this section to give you a clear picture on how things really are for you. Write down what you discover about yourself. For example, you may feel guilty doing or not doing something, you may feel a boost or lack of energy, you may get a headache or an ache somewhere. Try and document everything so that when you get to the third section, you will be able to make better decisions about what you need, what works for you and what does not.

In the third section, 'Creating My Plan', you will look for connections between what feels good and what doesn't and from this you will start creating your personal lifestyle plan.

In the fourth section, 'Let's Get Creative', you will create two vision boards on how you want to look and feel. Then you will create empowering statements to help you stick to your new vision of yourself.

We attract what we feel and what we think.

In the last section, 'Bring it all Together', you will create your magic story to enhance your vision and you will revise your chaser thoughts turning your negative thoughts into empowering thoughts. The last pages, 'Draw like a Child' and 'Write from Within', help you connect to your inner guidance, and to what is in your heart. I encourage you to play.

To get the most out of this journal, aim to complete the second section in one week and then take your time in the third, fourth and fifth sections by only completing a few pages at a time. Don't rush it. Think deeply about each question and see what comes to you and how it feels, then journal further on your thoughts. Keep in mind that your journal is a positive place, so write in a way that supports you and your efforts. Use each page to open your awareness and let your feelings guide you.

Two big things happen as you work through this journal. One, you get an honest snapshot of where you really are and two, you get the opportunity to create a lifestyle plan that is suited specifically to you.

> *Be aware how your body feels.*

Know that only you can make your life better. You decide on the changes you want to make and accept what you don't want to change. You are far better to make small changes that you can live with in the long run, than big changes that only last a few weeks. And remember to be kind to yourself. You can't change anything from the past, all you can do is choose to make each day better than yesterday.

Keep asking

> *Am I listening to my body? How do I feel right now?*

THOUGHTS

Write or draw your thoughts

I am Silent and Listen

When you stop and let your mind be still, even for a moment, you open a space that allows your inner child's voice to be heard.

To quieten your mind and bring it to stillness, simply take three deep breaths in and out. Focus on your breath and let your mind fall into a space that has no thoughts. When a thought floats in, observe it, then let it go as you bring your focus back to the breath.

FIND MOMENTS TO BE PRESENT

I can be silent and in the moment when I brush my teeth, have a shower, make the bed, or even as I am waiting for the jug to boil.

....
....
....
....
....
....
....
....
....

Download your free meditation www.rainbowvisionjournal.com/download

THOUGHTS

Write or draw your thoughts

Catching My Chaser Thoughts

As you work through each exercise, negative thoughts may pop into your head. What are you saying to yourself when you are not paying attention? Write whatever comes into your mind.

Do not analyse or change it, simply capture it here.

E.g. I can't do this, I'm no good, I'm too fat, I'm too unfit.

....
....
....
....
....
....
....
....
....
....
....
....

*When you are aware of your self-talk,
you can change whatever thoughts do not serve you.*

THOUGHTS

Write or draw your thoughts

Finding My Gold Nuggets

Capture any inspiring thoughts, words, sayings, memories or 'aha' moments that motivate or inspire you.

This makes up part of your pot of gold at the end of the rainbow.

- ....
- ....
- ....
- ....
- ....
- ....
- ....
- ....
- ....
- ....
- ....
- ....
- ....
- ....
- ....

I consciously choose to follow my dreams

THOUGHTS

Write or draw your thoughts

I am so Grateful for

Create a daily practice giving thanks for the things you already have, like the air you breath, the sun on your face, the ground you walk on, the food you eat, the eyes you see through, the nose you smell with. We have so much we take for granted each day. Being grateful allows you to see how truly blessed you already are in this moment.

WE ATTRACT WHAT WE FOCUS ON

....

....

....

....

....

....

....

....

....

....

....

....

Thank You, Thank You, Thank You.

*Start your vision from a place of gratitude
to manifest what you are seeking.*

WHERE I AM RIGHT NOW

What does well-being mean to you? Some of us enjoy sitting around, others enjoy being fit. Some like to eat healthily, and others like to indulge in the not-so-healthy foods and lifestyle. Write out what you think well-being is and circle on the scale below where you are at.

Next, record everything you do and feel in a typical week. Commit to seven days in a row to get an accurate picture. If you regularly eat out, have snacks and drinks, then include all these. Take special notice of how you feel throughout the day.

Column 1 – take notice if you ate because you were hungry or bored.

Column 2 – write everything you drink and the size.

Column 3 – list everything you eat and if it was a small, medium, or big portion.

Column 4, circle how you felt after eating and take notice of anything else your body tells you. Do you have a tight tummy, feel like a blob, have low energy, are your ankles swollen or your skin blotchy? Include any aches or pains you have during the day, any indigestion, any cravings, mood swings or anything else that feels either uncomfortable or great.

You will then summarise certain things about the day to give you an overall perspective on what you did and how that made you feel. This task can be a bit confronting because when we know we need to make changes we often avoid thinking about details. Just remember, you are who you are, and you can't change anything that has happened, so there is no need to beat yourself up about any bad habits. Simply take notice of anything that is not supporting you and choose that from now on. You are going to feel better. It all starts with a choice.

You will use this section as your base to create your lifestyle planner, so the more information you gather, the better your planner will suit you.

THOUGHTS

Write or draw your thoughts

Well-being and Daily Observations

**Well-being means different things to different people.
What does it mean to you?**

I believe well-being is ....
....
....
....
....

Now that you are clear on what well-being means to you, mark in RED pen how you see your own level of well-being on the scales below and use BLUE for where you would like it to be.

1	2	3	4	5	6	7	8	9	10
I am unfit									I am fit

1	2	3	4	5	6	7	8	9	10
I eat badly									I eat well

1	2	3	4	5	6	7	8	9	10
I constantly put myself down									I like who I am

1	2	3	4	5	6	7	8	9	10
I am always tired									I am full of energy

1	2	3	4	5	6	7	8	9	10
I am unhappy									I am happy

1	2	3	4	5	6	7	8	9	10
I hate my body									I love my body

DAY: Monday .... (Date)

Time Was I Hungry?	Drinks	What I Eat	How I feel after eating? Energy level 1 to 10
Breakfast	Coffee	• Large bowl milk and cereal • 2 toast, jam	Felt over full, sluggish 1 2 3 ④ 5 6 7 8 9 10
Breakfast .... am Y/N			1 2 3 4 5 6 7 8 9 10
Snack .... am Y/N			1 2 3 4 5 6 7 8 9 10
Lunch .... am/pm Y/N			1 2 3 4 5 6 7 8 9 10
Snack .... pm Y/N			1 2 3 4 5 6 7 8 9 10
Dinner .... pm Y/N			1 2 3 4 5 6 7 8 9 10
Extra Snacks .... am.pm Y/N			1 2 3 4 5 6 7 8 9 10

What thoughts did I have when eating?   Guilty | Rushed | Enjoyed

....

....

How many 250ml glasses of water did I drink today?   1 2 3 4 5 6 7 8 9 more

How many cups of coffee / soft drink / other did I drink today? 1 2 3 4 5 6 7 8 9

How many standard glasses of alcohol did I drink? 1 2 3 4 5 6 7 8 9 more

The exercise and movement I did today was ....

....

....

How I felt before doing it ....

....

How I felt after doing it ....

....

What level was my overall feeling of energy today? 1 2 3 4 5 6 7 8 9 10

What was my mood today?

Angry | Frustrated | Annoyed | Flat | Stressed | Anxious | Tired | Unwell
Good | Great | Happy | Energetic | Enthusiastic

How did I sleep last night?	Poor / Ok / Good / Great
What time of the day did I have the most energy?	Time .... am/pm
What time of the day did I have the least energy?	Time .... am/pm
When did I relax, have me time?	Time .... am/pm

What did I do? ....

....

Was there anything I felt I should have done today? Yes / No

What was it? ....

....

DAY: Tuesday .... (Date)

Time Was I Hungry?	Drinks	What I Eat	How I feel after eating? Energy level 1 to 10
Breakfast	Coffee	• Large bowl milk and cereal • 2 toast, jam	Felt over full, sluggish 1 2 3 ④ 5 6 7 8 9 10
Breakfast .... am Y/N			1 2 3 4 5 6 7 8 9 10
Snack .... am Y/N			1 2 3 4 5 6 7 8 9 10
Lunch .... am/pm Y/N			1 2 3 4 5 6 7 8 9 10
Snack .... pm Y/N			1 2 3 4 5 6 7 8 9 10
Dinner .... pm Y/N			1 2 3 4 5 6 7 8 9 10
Extra Snacks .... am.pm Y/N			1 2 3 4 5 6 7 8 9 10

What thoughts did I have when eating?   Guilty | Rushed | Enjoyed

....

....

How many 250ml glasses of water did I drink today?   1 2 3 4 5 6 7 8 9 more

How many cups of coffee / soft drink / other did I drink today?   1 2 3 4 5 6 7 8 9

How many standard glasses of alcohol did I drink?   1 2 3 4 5 6 7 8 9 more

The exercise and movement I did today was ....

....

....

How I felt before doing it ....

....

How I felt after doing it ....

....

What level was my overall feeling of energy today?   1 2 3 4 5 6 7 8 9 10

What was my mood today?

Angry | Frustrated | Annoyed | Flat | Stressed | Anxious | Tired | Unwell
Good | Great | Happy | Energetic | Enthusiastic

How did I sleep last night?	Poor / Ok / Good / Great
What time of the day did I have the most energy?	Time .... am/pm
What time of the day did I have the least energy?	Time .... am/pm
When did I relax, have me time?	Time .... am/pm

What did I do? ....

....

Was there anything I felt I should have done today?   Yes / No

What was it? ....

....

DAY: Wednesday .... (Date)

Time Was I Hungry?	Drinks	What I Eat	How I feel after eating? Energy level 1 to 10
Breakfast	Coffee	• Large bowl milk and cereal • 2 toast, jam	Felt over full, sluggish 1 2 3 ④ 5 6 7 8 9 10
Breakfast .... am Y/N			1 2 3 4 5 6 7 8 9 10
Snack .... am Y/N			1 2 3 4 5 6 7 8 9 10
Lunch .... am/pm Y/N			1 2 3 4 5 6 7 8 9 10
Snack .... pm Y/N			1 2 3 4 5 6 7 8 9 10
Dinner .... pm Y/N			1 2 3 4 5 6 7 8 9 10
Extra Snacks .... am.pm Y/N			1 2 3 4 5 6 7 8 9 10

What thoughts did I have when eating?   Guilty | Rushed | Enjoyed

....

....

How many 250ml glasses of water did I drink today?   1 2 3 4 5 6 7 8 9 more

How many cups of coffee / soft drink / other did I drink today?   1 2 3 4 5 6 7 8 9

How many standard glasses of alcohol did I drink?   1 2 3 4 5 6 7 8 9 more

The exercise and movement I did today was ....

....

....

How I felt before doing it ....

....

How I felt after doing it ....

....

What level was my overall feeling of energy today?   1 2 3 4 5 6 7 8 9 10

What was my mood today?

Angry | Frustrated | Annoyed | Flat | Stressed | Anxious | Tired | Unwell
Good | Great | Happy | Energetic | Enthusiastic

How did I sleep last night?	Poor / Ok / Good / Great
What time of the day did I have the most energy?	Time .... am/pm
What time of the day did I have the least energy?	Time .... am/pm
When did I relax, have me time?	Time .... am/pm

What did I do? ....

....

Was there anything I felt I should have done today?   Yes / No

What was it? ....

....

DAY: Thursday .... (Date)

Time Was I Hungry?	Drinks	What I Eat	How I feel after eating? Energy level 1 to 10
Breakfast	Coffee	• Large bowl milk and cereal • 2 toast, jam	Felt over full, sluggish 1 2 3 ④ 5 6 7 8 9 10
Breakfast .... am Y/N			1 2 3 4 5 6 7 8 9 10
Snack .... am Y/N			1 2 3 4 5 6 7 8 9 10
Lunch .... am/pm Y/N			1 2 3 4 5 6 7 8 9 10
Snack .... pm Y/N			1 2 3 4 5 6 7 8 9 10
Dinner .... pm Y/N			1 2 3 4 5 6 7 8 9 10
Extra Snacks .... am.pm Y/N			1 2 3 4 5 6 7 8 9 10

What thoughts did I have when eating?   Guilty | Rushed | Enjoyed

....

....

How many 250ml glasses of water did I drink today?   1 2 3 4 5 6 7 8 9 more

How many cups of coffee / soft drink / other did I drink today?   1 2 3 4 5 6 7 8 9

How many standard glasses of alcohol did I drink?   1 2 3 4 5 6 7 8 9 more

The exercise and movement I did today was ....

....

....

How I felt before doing it ....

....

How I felt after doing it ....

....

What level was my overall feeling of energy today?   1 2 3 4 5 6 7 8 9 10

What was my mood today?

Angry | Frustrated | Annoyed | Flat | Stressed | Anxious | Tired | Unwell
Good | Great | Happy | Energetic | Enthusiastic

How did I sleep last night?	Poor / Ok / Good / Great
What time of the day did I have the most energy?	Time .... am/pm
What time of the day did I have the least energy?	Time .... am/pm
When did I relax, have me time?	Time .... am/pm

What did I do? ....

....

Was there anything I felt I should have done today?   Yes / No

What was it? ....

....

DAY: Friday .... (Date)

Time Was I Hungry?	Drinks	What I Eat	How I feel after eating? Energy level 1 to 10
Breakfast	Coffee	• Large bowl milk and cereal • 2 toast, jam	Felt over full, sluggish 1 2 3 ④ 5 6 7 8 9 10
Breakfast .... am Y/N			1 2 3 4 5 6 7 8 9 10
Snack .... am Y/N			1 2 3 4 5 6 7 8 9 10
Lunch .... am/pm Y/N			1 2 3 4 5 6 7 8 9 10
Snack .... pm Y/N			1 2 3 4 5 6 7 8 9 10
Dinner .... pm Y/N			1 2 3 4 5 6 7 8 9 10
Extra Snacks .... am.pm Y/N			1 2 3 4 5 6 7 8 9 10

What thoughts did I have when eating?   Guilty | Rushed | Enjoyed

....

....

How many 250ml glasses of water did I drink today?   1 2 3 4 5 6 7 8 9 more

How many cups of coffee / soft drink / other did I drink today?   1 2 3 4 5 6 7 8 9

How many standard glasses of alcohol did I drink?   1 2 3 4 5 6 7 8 9 more

The exercise and movement I did today was ....

....

....

How I felt before doing it ....

....

How I felt after doing it ....

....

What level was my overall feeling of energy today?   1 2 3 4 5 6 7 8 9 10

What was my mood today?

Angry | Frustrated | Annoyed | Flat | Stressed | Anxious | Tired | Unwell
Good | Great | Happy | Energetic | Enthusiastic

How did I sleep last night?	Poor / Ok / Good / Great
What time of the day did I have the most energy?	Time .... am/pm
What time of the day did I have the least energy?	Time .... am/pm
When did I relax, have me time?	Time .... am/pm

What did I do? ....

....

Was there anything I felt I should have done today?   Yes / No

What was it? ....

....

DAY: Saturday .... (Date)

Time Was I Hungry?	Drinks	What I Eat	How I feel after eating? Energy level 1 to 10
Breakfast	Coffee	• Large bowl milk and cereal • 2 toast, jam	Felt over full, sluggish 1 2 3 ④ 5 6 7 8 9 10
Breakfast .... am Y/N			1 2 3 4 5 6 7 8 9 10
Snack .... am Y/N			1 2 3 4 5 6 7 8 9 10
Lunch .... am/pm Y/N			1 2 3 4 5 6 7 8 9 10
Snack .... pm Y/N			1 2 3 4 5 6 7 8 9 10
Dinner .... pm Y/N			1 2 3 4 5 6 7 8 9 10
Extra Snacks .... am.pm Y/N			1 2 3 4 5 6 7 8 9 10

What thoughts did I have when eating?   Guilty | Rushed | Enjoyed

....

....

How many 250ml glasses of water did I drink today?   1 2 3 4 5 6 7 8 9 more

How many cups of coffee / soft drink / other did I drink today?   1 2 3 4 5 6 7 8 9

How many standard glasses of alcohol did I drink?   1 2 3 4 5 6 7 8 9 more

The exercise and movement I did today was ....

....

....

How I felt before doing it ....

....

How I felt after doing it ....

....

What level was my overall feeling of energy today?   1 2 3 4 5 6 7 8 9 10

What was my mood today?

Angry | Frustrated | Annoyed | Flat | Stressed | Anxious | Tired | Unwell
Good | Great | Happy | Energetic | Enthusiastic

How did I sleep last night?	Poor / Ok / Good / Great
What time of the day did I have the most energy?	Time .... am/pm
What time of the day did I have the least energy?	Time .... am/pm
When did I relax, have me time?	Time .... am/pm

What did I do? ....

....

Was there anything I felt I should have done today?   Yes / No

What was it? ....

....

DAY: Sunday .... (Date)

Time Was I Hungry?	Drinks	What I Eat	How I feel after eating? Energy level 1 to 10
Breakfast	Coffee	• Large bowl milk and cereal • 2 toast, jam	Felt over full, sluggish 1 2 3 ④ 5 6 7 8 9 10
Breakfast .... am Y/N			1 2 3 4 5 6 7 8 9 10
Snack .... am Y/N			1 2 3 4 5 6 7 8 9 10
Lunch .... am/pm Y/N			1 2 3 4 5 6 7 8 9 10
Snack .... pm Y/N			1 2 3 4 5 6 7 8 9 10
Dinner .... pm Y/N			1 2 3 4 5 6 7 8 9 10
Extra Snacks .... am.pm Y/N			1 2 3 4 5 6 7 8 9 10

What thoughts did I have when eating?   Guilty | Rushed | Enjoyed

....

....

How many 250ml glasses of water did I drink today?   1 2 3 4 5 6 7 8 9 more

How many cups of coffee / soft drink / other did I drink today?   1 2 3 4 5 6 7 8 9

How many standard glasses of alcohol did I drink?   1 2 3 4 5 6 7 8 9 more

The exercise and movement I did today was ....

....

....

How I felt before doing it ....

....

How I felt after doing it ....

....

What level was my overall feeling of energy today?   1 2 3 4 5 6 7 8 9 10

What was my mood today?

Angry | Frustrated | Annoyed | Flat | Stressed | Anxious | Tired | Unwell
Good | Great | Happy | Energetic | Enthusiastic

How did I sleep last night?	Poor / Ok / Good / Great
What time of the day did I have the most energy?	Time .... am/pm
What time of the day did I have the least energy?	Time .... am/pm
When did I relax, have me time?	Time .... am/pm

What did I do? ....

....

Was there anything I felt I should have done today?   Yes / No

What was it? ....

....

THOUGHTS

Write or draw your thoughts

A Look at My Week

Take time to really think about how you felt.

Go back and circle in RED anything that made you feel uncomfortable, unhappy, guilty, or lethargic and use BLUE for anything that made you feel good. Then make a note of those things here.

Are there things that jump out showing a pattern or bad habits?

E.g. Did you get indigestion, headaches, joint pain, sleep poorly or something else more than once in the week? Did it happen when you ate something specific?

What is my body telling me that I should take notice of?

....
....
....
....
....
....
....
....
....
....
....
....

THOUGHTS

Write or draw your thoughts

How I Felt

How you felt each day will give you clues. At what times of the day did you feel best/worst? What were you doing? Write how you felt.

E.g. Happy, energised, guilty, rushed, pressured, tense, stressed, negative.

My eating ....
....

What I drank ....
....

My movement ....
....

How I felt / My moods ....
....

My sleeping ....
....

My energy levels ....
....

How I want to Feel

Write out how you want to feel differently in each of these areas?

Use the examples in brackets to give you ideas.

My eating (to feel good after eating)
....
....

What I drank (feel like my body is nourished, skin feels better)
....
....

My movement (to be fit enough to go on bush walks)
....
....

How I felt / My moods (positive, happy, do more things that I enjoy)
....
....

My sleeping (sleep a solid seven hours a night)
....
....

My energy levels (wake up full of energy)
....
....

Where do I Struggle?

Where do you really struggle? Is it the food you eat, the exercise, the lack of sleep, the not drinking enough water, an aching body, the lack of energy or the self-criticism?

What do I tell myself? (I can't sleep, my knee aches)

....
....
....
....
....
....
....

If I could change one thing, what would it be?

....
....
....
....
....
....
....

THOUGHTS

Write or draw your thoughts

What is My Indulgence?

Do you drink too many sugar drinks, eat too much, snack regularly, love sweets, ice creams or desserts, sleep in late, binge TV?

What I overindulge in is ....
....
....

Do I really love it or is it a habit? ....
....

What don't I want to give up? ....
....
....

What could I cut back? ....
....
....

Are there any foods or habits I could eliminate? ....
....
....

What could I replace them with? ....
....
....

Choosing what I Like

What are the things you felt good about?

My eating

....

....

What I drank

....

....

My movement

....

....

How I felt / My moods

....

....

My sleeping

....

....

My energy levels

....

....

THOUGHTS

Write or draw your thoughts

How is My Posture?

Think about how you stand and how you sit. Do you have good posture? What does your posture tell you? When you slouch you constrict your energy and your muscles. You give yourself unnecessary aches and pains and you appear to lack confidence.

Think about when you stand up tall. When you walk straight and with purpose. How do you feel compared to when you slouch? You may say you feel more comfortable slouching, but that is an excuse for a poor habit. Your body is not designed to slouch. Improving your posture when standing and sitting will greatly improve your well-being.

How do I sit?
....
....

How can I improve how I sit?
....
....

How do I stand?
....
....

How can I improve the way I stand?
....
....

THOUGHTS

Write or draw your thoughts

Creating New Habits

If you want to change anything in life, you must form new habits and that takes commitment. What can you change to feel better?

Use the examples in brackets to get ideas. Take baby steps in each area.

My eating, (smaller portions)

....
....

What I drink (two more glasses of water a day)

....
....

My movement (10 minute walk every day)

....
....

How I feel / My moods (have more me time, don't rush eating)

....
....

My sleeping (watch a funny show before bed)

....
....

My energy levels (eat less sugar)

....
....

An Honest Look

Does your body support you? Will it carry you through your life in a way that gives you quality of life or will it hold you back? Think about your eating and exercise habits and how your choices today are going to affect you in the next 5 to 10 years. Will you be happy with yourself if you keep doing what you are doing?

If you overeat now and you keep doing that, how big will you be? If you already have aches and pains or other issues, what will they be like?

If I change nothing in my lifestyle, what will my body be like in five years' time?

....

....

What about in 10 years' time?

....

....

How do I want my body to be in five years?

....

....

Am I living up to my definition of well-being?   YES / NO

If not, what do I need to change?

....

....

Am I prepared to make this change?   YES / NO

Journal Time

CREATING MY PLAN

We all know that there are things we could do to have better health, although it is one thing knowing it, and it is another thing doing it. In this section, you are going to make decisions on how you choose to improve your well-being in a way that is achievable for you. In a way that makes you feel strong.

Before you do that, it is important to get an understanding on how we humans sabotage our best intentions. Our subconscious mind is like a computer program. It doesn't feel or know what is right, it performs purely on its programming. What does this mean? It means that when we go to change a habit, our subconscious mind resists. The new habit is not part of our programming. It doesn't like change and will do what it can to keep things as they are.

Let me give you an example. Think about your computer. You open your emails, and you don't see it, but the programming is running in the background. Now say you want to paint a picture on your computer. You can't do it in your email program as it does not understand what you want. You need a different program, one that supports painting pictures. **You need a new program for your well-being.**

I can do this.

What does this mean to you? Say you want to lose 20kg. You have been overweight for some time and repeatedly tell yourself you are fat. Every time you look in the mirror or try on an outfit you say 'look how fat I am.' You decide to go on a diet. You do well for the first month and then you start to struggle, especially if you are eating foods you don't particularly like. Although you want to lose weight, your mind will do whatever it can to bring you back to the program that it knows 'I am fat.' In this case, back to the foods you ate before. You will have thoughts like, 'I'll just have this one piece of chocolate. I've been so good. I deserve a reward.' You will justify it to yourself until you give in because we use our weaknesses as our excuse.

Unfortunately, as soon as you give in to that self-talk, you have broken your momentum and your program is back running normally. The next day your mind says, 'I could have another piece of chocolate as that one yesterday didn't do any harm', and before you know it, you are back to square one. You have given up on your diet and gone back to your previous weight, if not more, and the worst thing is, you then give yourself a hard time for not succeeding! You feel unhappy because you are still fat, and that pulls your mood and energy down, and you feel useless because you can't seem to stick to anything. All this because your mind believes in the old program, that you are fat, because this is what you have told yourself for so long.

It is the same for anything you are trying to achieve. If you tell yourself you hate exercise, you won't last long going to the gym. If you say, 'I can't...' for anything, then guess what, you can't! We then compound this problem by how we feel. When we feel annoyed with ourselves for not succeeding, this emotion is strong. When we do succeed at something, we don't usually reward ourselves or pat ourselves on the back. Which feeling is generally stronger? The feeling of annoyance is stronger because we put a lot more focus and energy into it.

What if you changed how you thought and how you felt? What if you decided you needed a new way of thinking, a new program, because the way you have been thinking up until now, no longer serves you?

How we think, then how we feel is the basis of the law of attraction.

Whatever we think about and focus on, is what we get. This is the law of attraction and it is always working. Unfortunately, it is usually working against us as demonstrated above. Once we understand this, we can break our negative beliefs and turn them into ones that empower us. You will look at this further in My Self-Talk. What you capture on that page should be transferred to your Chaser page at the beginning of the journal, so that you can revise these later.

*To understand the Law of Attraction better,
download and read the Free e-book
https://www.rainbowvisionjournal.com/free-ebook/*

As you can see, awareness of how you think and feel are the keys to your well-being and now that you have a clear idea on what you do each day, and what can sabotage you, it's time to create your plan.

You are going to start this section by creating a new vision of yourself. When we are clear on our goals, we can use this to stay focused. Make your goals specific, as shown in the example, as these will help you in the next step where you decide what foods you will eat and what type of exercise to do.

> *What are you choosing to give up and what are you choosing to keep?*

Next, you will look at your self-talk, feel-good and accountability, which is where you create your daily lifestyle plan.

Take notice of how you think about the changes you want to make and how they make you feel. Find solutions where you have little or no resistance. If you try to make changes that you can feel tension just from the thought, then they are not the changes for you at this time. Look for options that feel right for you.

> *I regularly check in with my body to see how I feel.*

Start your plan with baby steps. You want this to work so keep it simple and let yourself be guided on what to change now. Do things you know you can succeed in, then slowly add more changes as you feel your momentum growing. This is a plan for life, so let yourself have some of the things you love, in moderation, remembering that life is to be enjoyed.

> *I am worth the effort.*

Making changes in our life does take effort, but aren't you worth it? Isn't your quality of life worth it? Most people put more effort into planning a holiday then looking after themselves, yet the holiday is over quickly, and our body stays with us for a lifetime! Choose to make your life better by staying focused on your goals and keeping your momentum and accountability going every day.

Visualisation Exercise

This little exercise helps you gain clarity on how you will look and feel as the healthy, happy person you aspire to be.

Put on some relaxing music to help block any distractions.

- Find a nice quiet spot, get comfortable, close your eyes, and allow yourself to relax.
- Take three big, deep breaths, in through the nose and out through the mouth. Blow out your tension and feel yourself relax with each breath.
- Keep breathing this way as you allow yourself to let go of any distractions. Focus on your breath connecting you to your heart.
- Let your mind wonder over what well-being means to you and see yourself as you are now.
- Now let your mind create an image of how you want to be.
- What would you change? How do you look? What are you wearing? How do you move? What is your posture like? How fit are you? What foods do you eat? What do you think of yourself? What do you do for fun? How do you feel within yourself and how do you feel about yourself?
- Get a strong image and believe you can be this person now. Feel it throughout your body.
- Let your mind wonder over the changes you made to be this vision.
- Put a smile on your face and tell yourself how great you are.
- Let the feeling of love, happiness, and excitement float all around you and notice how at peace you feel within yourself.
- Hold onto that feeling as you come back to awareness and open your eyes.
- Notice how you feel and start writing your vision on the next page.

Download the visualization recording and get clear on your vision.
http://www.rainbowvisionjournal.com/downloads

My Vision for Me

Think about all your answers in the first section along with what well-being means to you now and in the next 5-10 years. Write out how you would like to see yourself as if you have already achieved this vision.

What do you look like? What are you wearing? How do you move? What do you eat? What do you think of yourself? What do you do for fun? How do you feel about yourself?

....
....
....
....
....
....
....
....
....
....
....
....

Looking at the above answers, what are your top two goals? E.g. I am my ideal weight of x, and I can walk along bush tracks with ease.

1) ....
2) ....

My Eating Plan

Look back over your 7-day observation and where you struggled. List the various foods you will choose to eat at each mealtime. These will help you create a weekly eating plan. Remove everything from your home that is not on this list so that you remove temptation.

My Breakfast Food and Drink Options

E.g. One egg on one toast, small smear of butter, one coffee, one water

My Lunch Food and Drink Options

E.g. Stir-fried vegies with small tin of salmon, de cafe coffee, water

My Dinner Food and Drink Options

E.g. Small steak with my chosen salad and air-fried chips, cup of tea

My Snack Food and Drink Options (My small indulgences)

E.g. One homemade iced coffee (store ones have too much sugar)

*Create a shopping list each week.
Only buy what is on your list and never shop when you are hungry.*

My Movement Plan

There are lots of ways to move and exercise your body and these create part of your well-being, both mentally and physically. Think about activities you enjoy and do something that interests you.

If you like the water, join a swim club or aqua aerobics. If you like walking, ask a friend to join you, explore your neighbourhood, walk someone's dog, or go on bush walks. If you like dancing, learn a new style, join Zumba or dance around your house as you do chores. If you like company or support, join yoga, Pilates or a gym.

I like ....

....

I can see myself doing ....

....

....

Set your Intention:

I (be specific) ....

....

Every (how often) ....

Three examples: I do five minutes of stretches and a fifteen minute walk around my local area with my friend every Monday, Wednesday and Friday morning. Or, I do five minute leg and ankle stretches and five minute arm and upper body exercises every morning as soon as I get up. Or, I choose to join a gym and do their yoga class on Tuesday and Thursday nights and I bush walk 5km on Saturdays.

My Self-Talk

How you think about yourself means success or failure. When you are unhappy with yourself, you create tension in your body. Catch everything that you say to yourself that does not support your goals.

My challenges are ....

How I plan to work around my challenges ....

....

What I complain about (*add these to your Chaser page*)

....

....

I feel guilty when ....

....

How can I release the guilt? ....

....

I don't like my (eyes, legs, hair, nose, figure, weight) ....

....

Can I change any of these things?   Yes / No

If Yes, how can I change them? ....

....

If no, how can I let it go so I stop thinking about it? (by focusing on what we can't change, all we do is make ourselves unhappy) ....

....

My Feel-Good Plan

When you are joyful, your body is relaxed, therefore the key is to feel good about yourself. The more you love and appreciate yourself the better you feel. Find the things that make you feel good.

I feel happy when ....
....

I feel full of energy when ....
....

I feel confident when ....
....

I have ME Time (when/how often?) ....
....

The things I do for ME Time are ....
....
....

The positive things I tell myself ....
....
....

What I love about myself ....
....
....

We are what we think.

My Accountability Plan

To help create new lifestyle habits, set up a daily accountability plan. Only tell people who will support you. You may have a friend who also wants to create new habits, so work together and support each other.

Create a 30-day plan. Photocopy sheets as required. Put your daily sheet in a place where you can see it throughout the day to keep you on track. Within 14 days you will see changes. Write down the changes you notice to help keep you focused. Take a photo of yourself on the same day every month, so that you can look back and see those changes. Notice your skin, your smile, your posture, and how you move. Above all, notice how good you feel.

Example:

Day 1   Date: 20 May 21

My Goals: *My ideal weight is x, and I can walk bush tracks with ease*

My Plan today is

Breakfast	One egg on one toast, small smear of butter
Lunch	Stir fried vegies with small tin of salmon, cup of tea
Dinner	Small steak with my chosen salad and air-fried chips
Drinks	Five glasses of water, two coffees, two herbal teas
Movement	Five minutes stretches and 10 minute walk
Feel good	One homemade iced coffee, my reward from yesterday. Sat under a tree for 10 minutes me time.

Today I celebrate achieving: I ignored the urge to eat an ice cream
Did I stay on track to my goals? Yes
How I plan to reward myself?   an extra 15 minutes to doodle in my journal

Day .... Date: ....

My Goals: 1) ....

2) ....

My Plan today is

Breakfast	
Lunch	
Dinner	
Drinks	
Movement	
Feel good	

Today I celebrate achieving: ....

....

Have I stayed on track with my goals?   Yes / No

If yes, how I plan to reward myself: ....

....

If no, how do I feel about that? ....

....

Join the private Facebook Group
'Creating Vision Journals Together' for extra support.

Day .... Date: ....

My Goals: 1) ....

2) ....

My Plan today is

Breakfast	
Lunch	
Dinner	
Drinks	
Movement	
Feel good	

Today I celebrate achieving: ....

....

Have I stayed on track with my goals?   Yes / No

If yes, how I plan to reward myself: ....

....

If no, how do I feel about that? ....

....

Join the private Facebook Group
'Creating Vision Journals Together' for extra support.

Day .... Date: ....

My Goals: 1) ....

2) ....

My Plan today is

Breakfast	
Lunch	
Dinner	
Drinks	
Movement	
Feel good	

Today I celebrate achieving: ....

....

Have I stayed on track with my goals?   Yes / No

If yes, how I plan to reward myself: ....

....

If no, how do I feel about that? ....

....

Join the private Facebook Group
'Creating Vision Journals Together' for extra support.

Day .... Date: ....

My Goals: 1) ....

2) ....

My Plan today is

Breakfast	
Lunch	
Dinner	
Drinks	
Movement	
Feel good	

Today I celebrate achieving: ....
....

Have I stayed on track with my goals?   Yes / No

If yes, how I plan to reward myself: ....
....

If no, how do I feel about that? ....
....

Join the private Facebook Group
'Creating Vision Journals Together' for extra support.

Day .... Date: ....

My Goals: 1) ....

   2) ....

My Plan today is

Breakfast	
Lunch	
Dinner	
Drinks	
Movement	
Feel good	

Today I celebrate achieving: ....

....

Have I stayed on track with my goals?   Yes / No

If yes, how I plan to reward myself: ....

....

If no, how do I feel about that? ....

....

Join the private Facebook Group
'Creating Vision Journals Together' for extra support.

Day .... Date: ....

My Goals: 1) ....

2) ....

My Plan today is

Breakfast	
Lunch	
Dinner	
Drinks	
Movement	
Feel good	

Today I celebrate achieving: ....

....

Have I stayed on track with my goals?   Yes / No

If yes, how I plan to reward myself: ....

....

If no, how do I feel about that? ....

....

Join the private Facebook Group
'Creating Vision Journals Together' for extra support.

Day .... Date: ....

My Goals: 1) ....

2) ....

My Plan today is

Breakfast	
Lunch	
Dinner	
Drinks	
Movement	
Feel good	

Today I celebrate achieving: ....

....

Have I stayed on track with my goals?   Yes / No

If yes, how I plan to reward myself: ....

....

If no, how do I feel about that? ....

....

Join the private Facebook Group
'Creating Vision Journals Together' for extra support.

Journal Time

THOUGHTS

Write or draw your thoughts

LET'S GET CREATIVE

Creating a visual of your dream-self and looking at that visual regularly, is a powerful way to keep focused on what you want to achieve. It also helps you FEEL connected to your vision, especially when you combine it with empowering statements.

In this section you are encouraged to be creative as these exercises help your subconscious mind accept and support your new vision. On the next couple of pages are examples of words and statements to use as prompts. Choose anything that feels right for you as you create a set of your own personalized affirmation cards to use as a daily reminder of your vision.

Next, you will look at ways to create space to feel good each day. Your feelings attract what you desire so create a mind map, then vision board of all the things that make you feel good. From there you will look at creating a morning routine and a calendar to remind you of the things you are choosing for your new vision.

Create the vision of who you want to be.

Now you are ready to create a vision board of yourself. One where you look and feel good. Go back to the last section and re-read what you wrote in My Vision for Me, then redo the visualisation exercise, capturing how you want to look, act, and feel. Imagine you have succeeded in your plan and show it on your vision board.

Use the relaxation technique and draw a mandala as shown, to remove any stress and resistance you may feel at any time. The law of attraction is always working on the strongest feelings you have at any one time, so put yourself into a good mood prior to starting any of these exercises. Focus on feeling happy, excited, and grateful so those wonderful feelings flow onto your page. You are allowed to be happy and have fun, so relax and let yourself play.

YELLOW Words

Circle the words that you resonate most with

Joy	Forgiveness	Friendship	Compassion
Alert	Family	Nature	Fresh Air
Walking	Jogging	Stretching	Exercise
Healthy	Relaxed	Slim	Light
Playful	Bright	Laughter	Smile
Wisdom	Energy	Knowledge	Philosophy
Fit	Supple	Playful	Breathe
Water	Habits	Flexible	Movement
Summer	Spring	Flowers	Sunshine
Butterflies	Rebirth	Life	Happiness
Clean	Activity	Inspiration	Confidence
Pineapple	Lemon	Banana	Peach
Weight	Optimism	Spontaneous	Stimulation
Satisfaction	Youthful	Power	Thought
Daffodil	Sunflower	Dandelion	Buttercup
New Vision	Affirmations	Self-love	Acceptance

YELLOW Thoughts

Create statements that feel right for you

Every day my body gets stronger, healthier and happier	I am strong
I choose to be healthy	I love myself
I live a life of love and gratitude	I am worthy
Smiling sends a message to my brain to relax	I am free to be me
I embrace my uniqueness	I do what feels right for me
I accept who I am now	I am awesome
When I think good thoughts, I feel good	I am safe
I am allowing myself to be a happy person	I love and honour myself
I surround myself with people who make me feel good and raise my vibration	I choose to be me
I have decided to become the person I want to be	I get what I focus on
All change begins with a brave decision	I am vibrational energy
Love and happiness are already within me	I deserve ME time
I treat myself how I expect others to treat me	I am grateful
My body is my best friend	I trust myself
I have unconditional love for myself	I create my lifestyle

THOUGHTS

Write or draw your thoughts

My Empowering Affirmations

Create a set of personalised affirmation cards to use as daily support for your vision. Each day look at one card and say the affirmation over and over throughout the day. Journal on it, focusing on how this affirmation is strengthening your life. Feel the lovely energy of it go through you.

Look at your Self-talk and Catching My Chaser Thoughts' pages. How can you turn these thoughts into ones that support you and make you feel good?

E.g. 'I'm fat' becomes 'Every day I get closer to my ideal weight.'

Materials to create your cards

- A3 or A4 lightweight card (200 to 500gsm)
- Pens and paints or colouring in pencils
- A list of the sayings you want to use

Create Backgrounds

- Splash on paint or colour to create interesting backgrounds.
- Cut your card into equal size (A4 = 10 cards).
- When dry, write your empowering statements. E.g. I am a good person, I am in alignment with my vision of myself, I am happy, I am loving, I am ME and the only one in this world, I choose to be the vision I have for myself.

When we say I AM, we give ourselves more power, so create as many 'I am' statements as you can. You can also use 'I choose' 'I love', 'I attract' or 'I have' to start your statements. You can use sayings or famous quotes that really resonate with you. Do not use 'I want' (you don't want to keep wanting) and be careful you don't create negative statements like 'I am trying to be better at ...' This statement keeps you trying. It is not a positive affirmation.

Creating Space for ME Mind Map

Feeling good is important to your well-being so compile a list of what feels right for you and then create time in your schedule for these things.

No matter how busy you are, you can put on music, sing out loud, dance around the room or visualise what makes you happy.

Example

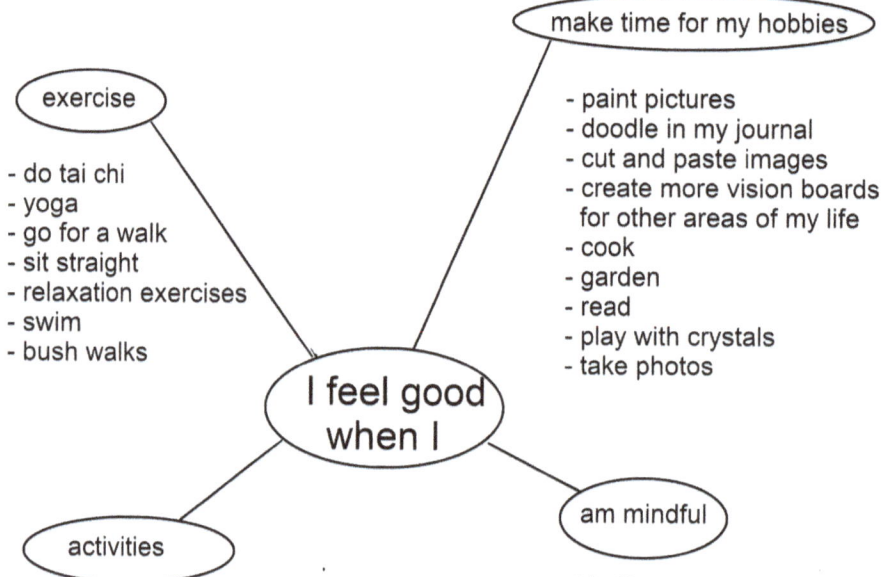

exercise
- do tai chi
- yoga
- go for a walk
- sit straight
- relaxation exercises
- swim
- bush walks

make time for my hobbies
- paint pictures
- doodle in my journal
- cut and paste images
- create more vision boards for other areas of my life
- cook
- garden
- read
- play with crystals
- take photos

I feel good when I

activities
- sit under a tree
- lie on the grass and watch clouds
- smell flowers
- bird watch
- connect to nature
- water the garden
- go for a swing
- play with kids or grandkids
- stroke the cat
- talk to the dog
- give yourself a massage

am mindful
- Meditate
- read my affirmations
- look at my vision board
- journal good things
- Wake and do my morning routine
- am grateful for everything in my life
- visualise being happy, full of love, energised
- be in the present moment
- focus on my inner peace

Create your own Mind Map

Blank Calendar

Sunday	Monday	Tuesday	Wednesday	Thursday	Friday	Saturday

Create a Calendar

It is great to have good intentions on how you plan to look after yourself, however, without action, these plans are only dreams.

Look at your mind map and choose the activities you want to do every day, every week, or every month.

Put a red tick by the daily activities, a blue tick by the weekly activities and a black tick by the monthly activities, then go to your phone or your calendar and put them in with reminders so that you do them.

Life gets busy and the first thing that gets dropped off is your self-care, yet it is the last thing you should let go.

If you are short of time, ask yourself why are you so busy? Are you doing things you love or are you doing things you feel you should do? What can you drop off your daily to-do list so that you can have more time to do what you love?

Can you get up 15 minutes earlier? Can you combine other tasks, so you have free time? Can you enlist your family's help. Can you include them in some of your activities? Ask yourself, what is the point of being busy if I am not enjoying my life? Make changes to de-stress your life and have more quality time with yourself.

Create a daily and weekly routine and put it in your calendar.

Make a commitment to yourself to ensure you do as many of the things that you love as you can.

Feel Good Technique

When you first wake in the morning, before getting out of bed or looking at your phone, give yourself an energy recharge so you start your day feeling good. You can also finish your day this way.

- When you wake, don't open your eyes.
- Feel how your body is; are you relaxed or stiff?
- Take a few deep breaths, keeping your eyes closed. If you are sore or stiff, breathe into that area and imagine it letting go and relaxing.
- Let your body feel relaxed all over.
- Think about all the things you are grateful for and let that build up your energy vibration. Being grateful makes us feel good.
- Think about your day ahead. Think about what you have to do, think only good thoughts. If you have challenges in your day, visualize yourself doing these things with ease and without feeling stressed. See it unfold in the way that is best for you.
- See solutions to any problems and feel yourself achieving everything you choose today.
- Put your hand over your heart and whisper to yourself your favourite affirmations (I am successful, I can do this).
- See yourself having a wonderful day, then when you are ready, open your eyes and get up.

The more you take time to feel good the more your inner happiness expands and the more you feel love and appreciation for yourself. When you let go of how you think you should be, accept how you are and focus only on feeling great about the life and body you have, your whole world will change. The truth is, happiness is a feeling that comes from within. It is a choice to make each day. It is our limiting beliefs that make us think happiness comes from how we look.

Create a routine to feel-good by setting up reminders in your calendar.

Creating My Mood Vision Board

You are going to create two vision boards in this journal.

**This first vision board is about how you feel and
the second one is about how you look.**

This feel vision board represents how you spend your time and what you do or would like to do that makes you feel good. Set an intention for your board, something like, 'I am creating this board to represent all the things that make me feel great.'

You may want to include images of

- anything from your mind map
- having massages or beauty treatments
- going to shows or concerts
- travelling to your favourite places
- going for walks on the beach
- enjoying a meal out
- visiting family and friends
- having or going to dinner parties

*Let your imagination go wild and add
anything that makes you feel great.*

Find a picture of yourself, one that makes you feel good, to put yourself into your vision. Include any empowering words or affirmations that feel right for you.

Once you have all your images, scatter them around until you have a layout that appeals to you. Stick them into place and add your words.

Once your board is completed, look at it regularly and believe in the new you.

My well-being vision board

THOUGHTS

Write or draw your thoughts

Creating the New ME Vision Board

Find images that reflect your new vision. It is immensely powerful to include an image of yourself. That way you are putting yourself 'in the picture', and therefore into your vision. Stick your face onto a body you like. Make it as real as you can. If anything feels impossible, remove it, and find a more generic image so that you can believe in it.

For example, say you want to be your ideal weight, but you are very overweight and just can't imagine yourself slim, then go for an easier fit. Look for an image that is halfway between where you are now and where you want to be. Remember we do things in baby steps.

The last vision board was about all the things that make you feel good.

This vision board is about how you want to look and be.

Include images that show
- the clothes you will wear
- how your body will look (put your face on the image)
- the types of foods you will eat
- any type of exercise you will do
- any other activity that is in alignment with your goals

Include a photo of yourself where you feel great, and it makes you smile when you look at it. Include any empowering words or affirmations that feel right for you.

Once your board is completed, look at it regularly and believe in the new you.

The best medicine for a healthy life is sunshine, water, good diet, rest, exercise, fresh air, love and positive self-talk.

My New ME Vision Board

THOUGHTS

Write or draw your thoughts

Relaxation Technique

Some days are stressful, and it is important to release that stress from your mind and your body. A simple relaxation technique can take just a few minutes to do yet it will improve how you feel immensely. Ideal to do when you go to bed at night, or you can do it sitting up at any time.

1. Lie comfortably and gently close your eyes.

2. Take a few deep breaths.

3. Focus on your toes, squeeze them, then relax. Focus on your ankles, squeeze, and relax. Your lower legs, squeeze and relax. Your upper legs, squeeze and relax. Focus on your bottom, squeeze it, and relax. Your stomach, squeeze and relax. Your chest, squeeze and relax. Your lower back, squeeze and relax. Your upper back, squeeze and relax. Your fingers, squeeze and relax. Your hands squeeze and relax. Your lower arms, squeeze and relax. Your upper arms, squeeze and relax. Your shoulders, squeeze and relax. Your neck, squeeze and relax. Your face, squeeze and relax. Your head, squeeze and relax.

4. Slowly count backwards from 20 to one and breath nice relaxing breaths.

5. Scan your body from head to toe with your mind and feel if there is any tension still in your body. If you find tension, focus on that spot, and say, 'I now release all tension as it no longer serves me.'

6. Visualise yourself in a nice relaxing place and let that image and feeling float throughout your body to relax further. Say 'I am relaxed.'

7. Keep breathing gently and keep relaxing as you visualise your serenity.

Sweet dreams.

DRAW A MANDALA

Create a Mandala

Mandala's are used for meditation, prayer, healing, art therapy and as a tool to simply be in the present moment and reduce stress and anxiety. You can create your own mandala or do a Google search and find hundreds of designs. The drawing and colouring of a mandala allows you to let go of stress and connect to your creative side.

Mandalas do not need to be perfect, when used for fun and stress relief.

Journal Time

BRING IT ALL TOGETHER

Now that you have a good idea on what well-being means to you and you have a vision in your mind on how that looks and feels, let's take it one step further. On the next pages you will create a story for yourself and your well-being vision.

Write your story and pretend you have a magic wand and three wishes. Put in as much detail as you can to really feel yourself in this story. What do you look like? How do you feel within your body? How do you feel about your body now? Who is with you? What are you doing? Imagine the steps you took to get to this amazing vision. Write your story as if you are already there and looking back, remembering what you have achieved. Let the vision unfold in as much detail as possible. Imagine it in all its glory.

> I believe in myself.

Remember, happiness is in every step along the way, not just in the end result. When you think from happiness, being happy becomes a part of your life no matter where you are on your journey. If you think you will only be happy when you get to your vision, then you are thinking from a place where you are lacking happiness and so you will always lack happiness. Feeling happy with yourself is a key component to manifesting your vision. Capture happiness in your writing. Use descriptive and emotional words to set the scene. If you are not happy, pretend. Make it up. Keep thinking happiness and you will start to feel it.

Once you have your magic story, then it is time to revise your chaser statements, turning them into empowering thoughts that support you, and then rewriting your magic story. Although this may feel like you are doubling up, these steps will give you even more clarity and determination as you move closer still to the well-being vision you are wanting to manifest into your life.

THOUGHTS

Write or draw your thoughts

It's Magic

You have a magical wand, and you have three wishes. Use your goals to guide you on your three wishes and create a fairytale story, using your imagination as if you have all three wishes now.

Where are you? What does it look like? What does it feel like? Who is with you? What are you doing? Describe the excitement that you feel as you are living your three dreams.

Before writing, take time to be still and go within. Feel yourself full of gratitude for all the wonderful things you already have, then ask your inner child to help select three wishes so you can write your fairytale.

Wishes

1) ....

2) ....

3) ....

....

....

....

....

....

....

> *Life is magical when I live in the high energy vibrations of love and gratitude.*

Revising My Chaser Thoughts

Go back to your Chaser page and have a good look at what you have captured. These are the thoughts that stop us doing what we want in life. They come from your belief system and outside influences from when you were very young. None of them are true, although they seem true when you hear them because they are familiar to you.

A thought from your heart, from your inner self, is always loving and supportive, NEVER negative. A thought from your mind is usually judgemental, criticising or disempowering in some way. It is simply how the subconscious mind gets programmed.

To understand this better, download the Rainbow Vision Journal free eBook.

Look at each chaser thought and see if there are any recurring patterns or themes. Then take each thought and create an empowering statement from it. E.g. I can't do this, can become, I am able to achieve what my heart desires.

Old thought ....
....

New empowering thought ....
....

Old thought ....
....

New empowering thought ....
....

Old thought ....

....

New empowering thought ....

....

Old thought ....

....

New empowering thought ....

....

Old thought ....

....

New empowering thought ....

....

Old thought ....

....

New empowering thought ....

....

Old thought ....

....

New empowering thought ....

....

Old thought ....

....

New empowering thought ....

....

Old thought ....

....

New empowering thought ....

....

Old thought ....

....

New empowering thought ....

....

THOUGHTS

Write or draw your thoughts

The Magic Rewritten

Now that you have revised your chaser thoughts and seen what is holding you back, go back and relook at your magical story with your three wishes.

Rewrite your magical story using your new empowering statements. Make your magical story powerful by weaving your new affirmations through it. You have the wand. You have the ability to create your life however you choose. So, what do you choose now? Ask yourself if it feels right for you. This is the most important question. The better it makes you feel, the more it is your true alignment so embrace it. Do not think about how your magical story will happen, only what it is like once you are there.

Believe in the magic of your story and trust that once you are clear on what you really what, it will come to you in ways you would never expect.

Before you rewrite your story, stop and ask for guidance. What is your heart telling you?

> *E.g. where you may have written 'I wish' or 'I want', change your words to 'I have' or 'I enjoy'. Remember you can say what you want, so long as it is uplifting – you have the magic wand!*

....

....

....

....

....

....

....

3 Action Steps

Look at your well-being plan, the new vision of yourself and your magical story. What 3 actions can you do right now to start bringing your number one goals into fruition? Insert each step into your calendar and set reminders to stay focused. Remember all new habits take time.

👣 ....
....
....
....

👣 ....
....
....
....

👣 ....
....
....
....

This is my commitment to myself and my well-being.

I wear YELLOW to remind myself of my commitment.

THOUGHTS

Write or draw your thoughts

My Reward

How will you reward yourself once you have completed all three steps?

Make your reward something that you would not normally do for yourself so that when you have completed your three steps, you feel excited and enjoy your reward. Then use your excitement to create another three steps and keep your momentum going.

What will happen if I don't complete my steps? How will I feel?

....

....

....

Check In

How do you feel now that you have created a well-being plan that suits you? Do you feel happier than when you started your journal? Remember life is a journey. You cannot change things overnight. This is a journey into well-being so that you can do, be and have a FABuLous life. This is a plan for your whole life, so that you can enjoy your life as much as possible.

The more you choose to be true to yourself, the happier you become. No one has the power to make you happy, except you. Choose to be happy by choosing to live from your heart and do what makes your heart sing.

The steps you have learnt in this journal can be applied to everything in your life, not just your well-being. It is the same process. Decide what is important and why. Get clear on how it feels, imagine it is real for you right now and write out that story. Believe in your vision, be thankful for it, feel the happiness of it flow through you and allow it to come to you however it unfolds and allow yourself to enjoy the journey.

It really is all up to you.

You can have a lovely magical life, it's not hard, it just takes a bit of effort and commitment on your behalf. The great thing is, you have the power to choose. Sometimes it may not seem that way, but you do, even when things are out of your control. You still have the power to choose how you will react, and how you will think and how you will talk to yourself. You can choose to be stressed and negative, or you can choose to be positive and as happy as you can in the situation. This is what determines your well-being and quality of life. Be honest with yourself and let your heart guide you.

Continue your creativity and inner connection as you draw and write on the next pages.

Journal Time – Keep up the Magic

*Happiness and well-being is about enjoying
who we are now and all that we have.*

What's Next?

The YELLOW Vision was the third journal in a series of seven steps to follow your heart and create your pot of GOLD.

The next step is GREEN – My Abundance.

How to attract money and abundance into your life.

GREEN is where you discover what you think about time and money, and how to make them flow to you in abundance.

To learn more about GREEN, visit
www.rainbowvisionjournal.com/green

Continue journaling to gain clarity on
what is right for you and practice every day to
draw like a child and write from within.

It really is the easiest way to learn how to follow your heart.

DRAW LIKE A CHILD

WRITE FROM WITHIN

DRAW LIKE A CHILD

WRITE FROM WITHIN

DRAW LIKE A CHILD

WRITE FROM WITHIN

DRAW LIKE A CHILD

WRITE FROM WITHIN

DRAW LIKE A CHILD

WRITE FROM WITHIN

DRAW LIKE A CHILD

WRITE FROM WITHIN

DRAW LIKE A CHILD

WRITE FROM WITHIN

DRAW LIKE A CHILD

WRITE FROM WITHIN

DRAW LIKE A CHILD

WRITE FROM WITHIN

DRAW LIKE A CHILD

WRITE FROM WITHIN

DRAW LIKE A CHILD

WRITE FROM WITHIN

DRAW LIKE A CHILD

WRITE FROM WITHIN

DRAW LIKE A CHILD

WRITE FROM WITHIN

DRAW LIKE A CHILD

WRITE FROM WITHIN

DRAW LIKE A CHILD

WRITE FROM WITHIN

DRAW LIKE A CHILD

WRITE FROM WITHIN

DRAW LIKE A CHILD

WRITE FROM WITHIN

DRAW LIKE A CHILD

WRITE FROM WITHIN

DRAW LIKE A CHILD

WRITE FROM WITHIN

DRAW LIKE A CHILD

WRITE FROM WITHIN

DRAW LIKE A CHILD

WRITE FROM WITHIN

DRAW LIKE A CHILD

WRITE FROM WITHIN

DRAW LIKE A CHILD

WRITE FROM WITHIN

DRAW LIKE A CHILD

WRITE FROM WITHIN

Accept the body you have and love it unconditionally.

Congratulations
on reaching the end of your journal

Well done! Now that you have completed all this in-depth work, don't let it slip away. Set up a daily ritual with the intention of topping up your energy vibration as a constant reminder to look after your well-being every day no matter what is transpiring in your life.

Remember, you have the power to choose your thoughts and your responses. When you choose to think and respond from love, you get love. When you choose to think from fear and guilt, you get fear and guilt.

Being aware of your thoughts and feelings then choosing to align them with your true heart's desire, is what creates a FABuLous life. You have the power to do it, you just need to believe in yourself and practice it for just five minutes every day. When you choose to make it a way of life that you cherish, it will become your life, and that is when the magic really happens.

Don't forget your free gifts on page ix

To receive further support on your self-empowerment journey,
join the private Facebook Group
Creating Vision Journals Together

The GREEN journal is next in this series and is about abundance. It is where you will decide how much money you really need and how you can have more time and less stress. These journals build on what is in your heart, starting with your love and support in RED, the dreams you have in ORANGE and the well-being you choose in YELLOW.

GREEN is where you get clear on what money you want and why.

Until we meet again, follow your heart and stay true to yourself.

NAMASTE
(I bow to the divine in you)

www.ingramcontent.com/pod-product-compliance
Lightning Source LLC
Chambersburg PA
CBHW061133010526
44107CB00068B/2922